Why Women Rule Better in Power

Embracing Feminine Leadership: Exploring the Notion of Why Women Rule Better in Power

Table of contents

Introduction

In recent decades, a paradigm shift has been unfolding in the realms of leadership, challenging traditional notions and paving the way for a more inclusive and diverse approach. One aspect gaining increasing recognition is the idea that women, when entrusted with positions of power, bring unique qualities and perspectives that can lead to more effective governance. This notion challenges centuries-old stereotypes and opens a dialogue on the advantages of embracing feminine leadership styles in various spheres of influence. Historically, societies around the world have predominantly been governed by men, reflecting deeply ingrained patriarchal structures. However, as we navigate the complexities of the 21st century, there is a growing acknowledgment that diverse leadership, inclusive of women, is not merely an act of social justice but a pragmatic choice for the betterment of societies. This introduction explores the compelling reasons behind the assertion that women rule better in power, delving into aspects of communication, empathy, collaboration, and long-term vision that are often associated with feminine leadership styles. Communication, a cornerstone of effective leadership, takes on a distinct quality when led by women. Studies suggest that women tend to employ more collaborative and inclusive communication styles, fostering an environment where diverse voices are heard and valued. This approach stands in contrast to more autocratic styles often associated with traditional male leadership. As societies become increasingly interconnected and globalized, the ability to navigate diverse perspectives and foster open dialogue becomes paramount. Women, with their inclination towards empathetic communication, create a conducive atmosphere for collaboration and innovation.

Empathy, a trait often associated with the feminine, is emerging as a critical component of successful leadership. Women in power tend to prioritize understanding the needs and concerns of those they lead, leading to more compassionate decision-making. This empathetic approach not only enhances workplace satisfaction but also contributes to the creation of policies that address the diverse needs of communities. In a world grappling with complex challenges such as climate change, inequality, and global health crises, leaders who prioritize empathy can forge a path toward sustainable and inclusive solutions. Collaboration, another strength inherent in many women leaders, challenges the conventional hierarchical model of decision-making. Women in power often seek consensus and input from various stakeholders, fostering a sense of shared responsibility. This collaborative approach is particularly relevant in the face of multifaceted challenges that demand interdisciplinary solutions. As we navigate an era marked by rapid technological advancements and interconnected global systems, leaders who prioritize collaboration can navigate the complexities more effectively.

Long-term vision, often associated with a more holistic and strategic approach, is a quality that women leaders frequently bring to the table. Studies suggest that women tend to focus on sustainable and long-term goals, considering the broader impact of their decisions. In contrast to short-term, profit-centric approaches that have been critiqued in various sectors, feminine leadership styles emphasize the importance of responsible and forward-thinking governance. This is particularly pertinent in addressing issues such as environmental sustainability, where immediate gains may conflict with the long-term well-being of the planet.

While the assertion that women rule better in power challenges entrenched gender stereotypes, it is essential to note that this perspective does not seek to essentialize or generalize the qualities of women. Instead, it calls for a recognition and celebration of the diverse leadership styles that women bring to the table. It acknowledges that effective leadership is not confined to gender but is shaped by a combination of individual qualities, experiences, and societal expectations.

In conclusion, this exploration sets the stage for a deeper examination of the advantages of feminine leadership in various spheres. As we grapple with complex challenges that demand innovative solutions, it becomes imperative to diversify our leadership models. Embracing the notion that women rule better in power is not just an act of progress but a pragmatic choice for building a more equitable, empathetic, and sustainable future.

Communication and Emotional Intelligence In Women

Communication and emotional intelligence play crucial roles in personal and professional success. In recent years, there has been growing interest in understanding how these aspects manifest in women. This exploration not only sheds light on gender dynamics but also underscores the unique strengths that women bring to interpersonal interactions and leadership roles.

Body:
Communication Styles:
Women often exhibit nuanced communication styles characterized by empathy, active listening, and collaboration. Research suggests that women tend to focus on building relationships, fostering open dialogue, and creating inclusive environments. These qualities contribute to effective teamwork and conflict resolution.
Verbal and Nonverbal Communication:
Women are known for their adeptness in both verbal and nonverbal communication. They often excel in articulating thoughts and emotions, using language to express empathy and build connections. Nonverbal cues, such as facial expressions and body language, are also areas where women demonstrate heightened sensitivity, enhancing their ability to convey and interpret emotions.
Empathy:
Emotional intelligence, a key component of effective communication, is exemplified in women through their high levels of empathy. The ability to understand and share others' feelings fosters strong interpersonal relationships, promotes a supportive work environment, and contributes to successful collaboration.
Adaptability:
Women frequently showcase adaptability in their communication styles, tailoring their approach based on the context and audience. This flexibility is a valuable asset in navigating diverse social and professional settings, enabling women to connect with others from various backgrounds.
Conflict Resolution:
Women often approach conflict resolution with a focus on understanding perspectives and finding mutually beneficial solutions. Their emphasis on collaboration and effective communication in resolving conflicts contributes to a positive and harmonious work atmosphere.
Leadership and Emotional Intelligence:
Emotional intelligence is a key factor in effective leadership. Women leaders, leveraging their emotional intelligence, often excel in creating supportive work environments, fostering team cohesion, and making sound decisions based on a deep understanding of emotions and interpersonal dynamics.
Challenges Faced:
Despite these strengths, women may encounter challenges in communication, including gender biases and societal expectations. Overcoming these hurdles requires acknowledging and addressing such biases to create more inclusive environments that recognize and appreciate diverse communication styles.
Cultural and Global Perspectives:

Women's communication and emotional intelligence are influenced by cultural contexts. Understanding these variations is essential in globalized settings, where effective communication across diverse cultures is paramount. Women's ability to navigate cultural nuances contributes to successful international collaborations.

Conclusion:
In conclusion, communication and emotional intelligence in women are powerful assets that contribute to positive interpersonal relationships, effective leadership, and successful collaboration. Recognizing and valuing the unique strengths that women bring to these areas fosters a more inclusive and dynamic social and professional landscape. As society continues to evolve, acknowledging and leveraging the diverse communication styles and emotional intelligence of women will undoubtedly lead to enhanced collective success.

Empathy in Leadership

Empathy in leadership is a crucial and often underestimated quality that can significantly impact the success and effectiveness of a leader. It involves the ability to understand and share the feelings of others, demonstrating genuine concern for their well-being. In the fast-paced and competitive world of business, empathy might seem like a soft skill, but its importance cannot be overstated.

Leaders who exhibit empathy create a positive and inclusive work environment. By understanding the needs and emotions of their team members, empathetic leaders foster a sense of belonging and trust. This, in turn, enhances collaboration and communication within the team, leading to increased productivity and job satisfaction.

Moreover, empathetic leaders tend to be better at resolving conflicts. By acknowledging and validating the emotions of those involved, they can address underlying issues and find solutions that satisfy everyone involved. This not only prevents lingering resentment but also strengthens the team's cohesion.

In times of change or crisis, empathy becomes even more critical. Leaders who can empathize with their team members during challenging periods build resilience and inspire loyalty. This emotional connection creates a support system that encourages individuals to navigate uncertainties with confidence, knowing that their leader understands and cares about their concerns.

Empathy is not just about understanding emotions; it also involves effective communication. Leaders who possess empathy can convey their thoughts and decisions in a way that resonates with the diverse perspectives within their team. This skill is particularly valuable in globalized workplaces where cultural differences play a significant role.

Furthermore, empathetic leaders are more attuned to the personal and professional development of their team members. They recognize individual strengths and weaknesses, providing tailored guidance and support. This personalized approach contributes to the growth of each team member, ultimately benefiting the entire organization.

However, striking the right balance is crucial. Leaders must be empathetic without compromising their objectivity or decision-making abilities. Being too empathetic might lead to indecisiveness, and leaders must find a middle ground to maintain authority while still fostering a supportive environment.

In conclusion, empathy is a foundational element of effective leadership. Leaders who prioritize understanding and connecting with their team members create a positive work culture, foster collaboration, and navigate challenges with resilience. In an ever-evolving business landscape, the significance of empathy in leadership cannot be overstated.

Collaborative Decision-Making

Collaborative decision-making is a dynamic process that involves multiple individuals or stakeholders working together to reach a consensus or make informed choices. This approach emphasizes collective intelligence, leveraging the diverse perspectives, expertise, and experiences of those involved. In this exploration of collaborative decision-making, we will delve into its key principles, benefits, challenges, and practical applications.

At its core, collaborative decision-making seeks to foster a sense of inclusivity and engagement among participants. By involving individuals with different backgrounds, skills, and knowledge, organizations can tap into a rich pool of ideas and insights. This diversity not only broadens the scope of potential solutions but also enhances the overall quality of decision outcomes.

One fundamental principle of collaborative decision-making is open communication. Establishing an environment where participants feel free to express their thoughts and opinions is crucial. This requires effective communication channels, active listening, and a culture that values each contributor's input. When individuals feel heard and respected, they are more likely to actively engage in the decision-making process.

Transparency is another key element of successful collaborative decision-making. Providing relevant information to all stakeholders ensures that decisions are based on a comprehensive understanding of the situation. This transparency builds trust among participants and fosters a shared commitment to the chosen course of action.

In addition to these principles, collaborative decision-making often involves structured methodologies to guide the process. One popular approach is consensus decision-making, where participants strive to reach an agreement that all can support. This method encourages compromise and ensures that decisions reflect the collective will, rather than being imposed by a minority.

The benefits of collaborative decision-making are manifold. One of the primary advantages is the ability to harness the collective intelligence of a group. By pooling diverse perspectives, organizations can uncover innovative solutions that may not be apparent in a traditional top-down decision-making model. This creativity and innovation are crucial in today's rapidly evolving business landscape.

Furthermore, collaborative decision-making enhances the sense of ownership and commitment among participants. When individuals are actively involved in the decision-making process, they are more likely to be invested in the successful implementation of the chosen course of action. This sense of ownership can lead to increased motivation and a stronger organizational culture.

Collaborative decision-making also promotes organizational learning. As participants share their knowledge and experiences, everyone involved gains insights that contribute to continuous improvement. This iterative learning process helps organizations adapt to changing circumstances and make more informed decisions in the future.

Despite its numerous advantages, collaborative decision-making comes with its own set of challenges. One common obstacle is the potential for conflict among participants. Differing opinions and perspectives may lead to disagreements that can impede the decision-making process. Effectively managing and resolving conflicts is crucial for maintaining a constructive collaborative environment.

Another challenge is the potential for decision-making to become time-consuming. Involving multiple stakeholders and reaching a consensus can take longer than decisions made by a single authority. Organizations must balance the benefits of inclusive decision-making with the need to make timely choices, especially in fast-paced industries.

To overcome these challenges, organizations can implement strategies to streamline the collaborative decision-making process. This may include establishing clear decision-making frameworks, providing training on effective communication and conflict resolution, and leveraging technology to facilitate virtual collaboration among geographically dispersed teams.

Practical applications of collaborative decision-making span various industries and contexts. In business settings, organizations often use this approach for strategic planning, project management, and product development. Engaging cross-functional teams in decision-making processes ensures that all relevant perspectives are considered, leading to more comprehensive and well-informed choices.

In the realm of public policy, collaborative decision-making is increasingly employed to address complex societal issues. Governments and community organizations recognize the value of involving citizens in decisions that directly impact their lives. This participatory approach enhances the legitimacy of policies and contributes to a more engaged and informed citizenry.

In healthcare, collaborative decision-making plays a crucial role in patient care. Shared decision-making between healthcare professionals and patients ensures that treatment plans align with patients' values and preferences. This patient-centered approach improves overall satisfaction and adherence to medical recommendations.

Educational institutions also benefit from collaborative decision-making, whether in curriculum development, faculty governance, or administrative decision processes. By involving various stakeholders, such as teachers, students, and parents, schools can create a more inclusive and effective learning environment.

In conclusion, collaborative decision-making is a powerful approach that leverages the collective intelligence of individuals to make informed choices. Emphasizing principles such as open communication, transparency, and structured methodologies, this model fosters creativity, ownership, and organizational learning. While challenges exist, implementing strategies to manage conflicts and streamline the decision-making process can enhance the effectiveness of collaboration. The practical applications of collaborative decision-making are diverse, spanning business, public policy, healthcare, and education. As organizations continue to navigate complex and dynamic environments, embracing collaborative decision-making is increasingly recognized as a key driver of success.

Ensuring Equal Opportunities

Ensuring equal opportunities is a fundamental aspect of fostering a just and inclusive society. This concept goes beyond mere legal compliance and extends to creating an environment where individuals, regardless of their background, have equitable access to resources, education, employment, and other opportunities.

To achieve equal opportunities, it is crucial to address various dimensions of diversity, including but not limited to race, gender, ethnicity, socio-economic status, and physical abilities. Policies and practices aimed at eliminating discrimination and bias play a pivotal role in creating a level playing field for everyone.

One key area in ensuring equal opportunities is education. By implementing inclusive educational policies, we can break down barriers that hinder access to quality education for certain groups. This includes providing financial support, creating diverse curricula, and fostering a supportive learning environment that acknowledges and celebrates differences.

Moreover, workplaces play a crucial role in shaping equal opportunities. Companies need to adopt fair hiring practices, promoting diversity at all levels, and providing equal pay for equal work. Cultivating an inclusive corporate culture not only enhances the overall work environment but also contributes to increased innovation and productivity.

Legislation is a powerful tool in the pursuit of equal opportunities. Anti-discrimination laws and affirmative action policies can help address historical inequalities and systemic biases. However, it is essential to regularly review and update these laws to ensure their relevance and effectiveness in a rapidly evolving society.

In addition to legal frameworks, public awareness campaigns and educational initiatives can challenge stereotypes and prejudices that contribute to unequal opportunities. Changing societal attitudes is a gradual process that requires collective efforts to reshape perceptions and promote a more inclusive mindset.

It is important to recognize that ensuring equal opportunities goes hand in hand with addressing economic disparities. Social and economic inequality often go hand in hand, and efforts to bridge the gap must involve measures that promote financial inclusivity and address systemic barriers to economic advancement.

Furthermore, technology can be leveraged to enhance equal opportunities. Access to digital resources and skills is becoming increasingly vital in today's world. Efforts should be made to bridge the digital divide, ensuring that individuals from all backgrounds have the necessary tools and skills to participate in the digital economy.

While progress has been made in many areas, challenges persist. Deep-rooted biases, both conscious and unconscious, continue to influence decision-making processes. Continuous education and training programs can help individuals and organizations recognize and overcome these biases, fostering a more inclusive and equitable society.

In conclusion, ensuring equal opportunities requires a multi-faceted approach that encompasses education, employment, legislation, societal attitudes, and technological advancements. It is a collective responsibility that demands continuous efforts to dismantle barriers and create a society where everyone has the chance to thrive and contribute to the best of their abilities.

Navigating Complexity

Navigating complexity is a multifaceted challenge that pervades various aspects of our personal, professional, and societal landscapes. In a world characterized by interconnected systems, rapid technological advancements, and intricate relationships, individuals and organizations must develop a nuanced understanding of complexity to thrive. This essay explores the concept of navigating complexity, examining its significance, strategies for effective navigation, and the implications for individuals and society.

Complexity manifests in diverse forms, encompassing intricate problems, dynamic environments, and interconnected variables. Whether in business, science, or daily life, individuals encounter challenges that defy simple solutions. Understanding complexity involves acknowledging the interconnectedness and interdependence of elements within a system. It requires embracing uncertainty, ambiguity, and the recognition that linear cause-and-effect relationships often fall short in capturing the intricacies of real-world scenarios.

Navigating complexity demands a shift from traditional, reductionist approaches to more holistic, systems thinking. Rather than breaking problems into isolated components, individuals must consider the interconnected web of relationships and feedback loops that contribute to the complexity of a situation. This perspective encourages a deeper exploration of underlying patterns, emergent behaviors, and the systemic nature of challenges.

In the realm of business, navigating complexity is a critical skill for leaders and organizations. Globalization, technological advancements, and the interconnectivity of markets have amplified the complexity of decision-making processes. Leaders must contend with a multitude of factors, from geopolitical issues to market dynamics, customer expectations, and internal organizational complexities.

Adopting a complexity mindset in business involves recognizing that traditional, linear approaches may not be effective in the face of intricate challenges. Decision-makers need to consider the broader context, anticipate unintended consequences, and be agile in responding to evolving situations. Embracing complexity also means fostering a culture that values adaptability, continuous learning, and collaboration.

Innovation, a key driver of progress, often emerges from the intersection of diverse ideas and disciplines. Navigating complexity in the realm of innovation involves creating environments that encourage cross-disciplinary collaboration, diverse perspectives, and the exploration of unconventional solutions. Embracing the complexity of innovation requires organizations to move beyond rigid structures and hierarchies, fostering a culture that values experimentation, learning from failures, and adapting to change.

Individuals, too, face complexity in their personal lives. Relationships, career decisions, and life choices are all influenced by a myriad of factors, making navigation through these complexities a constant challenge. Developing emotional intelligence, self-awareness, and a capacity for adaptability becomes crucial in managing personal complexities.

Education plays a pivotal role in preparing individuals to navigate complexity. Traditional educational models often emphasize specialization and siloed knowledge, but a more holistic approach is needed. Curricula should encourage interdisciplinary learning, critical thinking, and problem-solving skills that equip individuals to grapple with the complexities of the real world. Additionally, fostering a growth mindset, where individuals view challenges as opportunities for learning and growth, can enhance their capacity to navigate complexity.

Technological advancements, while contributing to the complexity of our world, also offer tools and solutions for navigating it. Artificial intelligence, data analytics, and other technologies can help in understanding complex patterns, predicting outcomes, and making more informed decisions. However, the responsible and ethical use of technology is paramount to ensuring that it serves as an enabler rather than a source of additional complexity.

The role of leadership in navigating complexity cannot be overstated. Leaders must not only possess a deep understanding of complexity but also exhibit the resilience and adaptability to lead in uncertain and dynamic environments. They should promote a culture that values learning, embraces diversity, and encourages open communication. A collaborative leadership style that leverages the collective intelligence of teams is particularly effective in navigating complexity.

In the context of societal challenges, such as climate change, geopolitical conflicts, and public health crises, navigating complexity becomes an urgent imperative. These challenges are characterized by their interconnected nature, transcending borders and disciplines. Solving them requires global cooperation, interdisciplinary approaches, and a shared commitment to sustainable and inclusive solutions.

Global organizations and institutions play a pivotal role in navigating societal complexity. Collaborative efforts, such as international partnerships, knowledge-sharing platforms, and coordinated responses to global challenges, become essential. Navigating complexity at the societal level also involves addressing issues of equity, justice, and inclusivity to ensure that solutions benefit all segments of the population.

In conclusion, navigating complexity is an inherent and pervasive aspect of our modern existence. It requires a shift in mindset, moving away from reductionist thinking towards holistic, systems-oriented approaches. Whether in business, personal life, education, or societal challenges, the ability to navigate complexity is a skill that individuals and organizations must cultivate. Embracing uncertainty, fostering a culture of continuous learning, and leveraging technology responsibly are crucial components of effective navigation. Ultimately, in a world characterized by intricate interdependencies, those who can navigate complexity adeptly are better positioned to thrive and contribute to positive, sustainable outcomes.

Empowering Others

Empowering others is a transformative process that involves providing individuals with the tools, resources, and support needed to take control of their lives and make meaningful decisions. This concept goes beyond mere delegation of tasks; it encompasses fostering a sense of autonomy, self-efficacy, and confidence within individuals. In this exploration of empowerment, we will delve into its significance, the various dimensions it encompasses, and the positive outcomes it can yield in personal and professional realms.

At its core, empowering others is about recognizing and respecting the unique capabilities and perspectives each person brings to the table. It involves creating an environment that values diversity, encourages collaboration, and promotes inclusivity. Empowerment is not a one-size-fits-all approach; instead, it requires a nuanced understanding of individual strengths, weaknesses, and aspirations.

One key aspect of empowerment is the development of effective communication skills. Clear and open communication establishes trust and transparency, crucial elements in any empowering relationship. Leaders, mentors, or individuals aiming to empower others must be adept at active listening, empathy, and providing constructive feedback. Through communication, people can express their ideas, concerns, and aspirations, fostering an atmosphere where everyone feels heard and understood.

Education plays a pivotal role in empowerment. By providing individuals with access to knowledge and skills, they gain the ability to make informed decisions and navigate various aspects of their lives. This could range from formal education to on-the-job training, mentorship programs, or skill-building workshops. The democratization of information through education is a powerful tool in breaking down barriers and leveling the playing field.

Empowering others also involves instilling a sense of accountability and responsibility. Encouraging individuals to take ownership of their actions and decisions fosters a proactive mindset. This shift from a passive role to an active participant contributes to personal growth and development. Moreover, it builds a culture of accountability within teams and communities, where each member understands their role in achieving collective goals.

Mentorship is a cornerstone of empowerment. A mentor serves as a guide, providing valuable insights, sharing experiences, and offering constructive guidance. Through mentorship, individuals can navigate challenges, set realistic goals, and gain a broader perspective on their potential. Mentorship relationships often transcend traditional hierarchical structures, creating a supportive network that empowers both mentor and mentee.

In the workplace, empowering leadership is gaining recognition as a driver of organizational success. Leaders who empower their teams foster a culture of innovation, creativity, and collaboration. By trusting employees with responsibilities and decision-making authority, leaders not only tap into the diverse talents within their teams but also cultivate a sense of ownership and commitment.

Empowerment extends beyond professional settings to community and social contexts. Grassroots initiatives that empower individuals to address local challenges, participate in decision-making processes, and advocate for their needs contribute to vibrant and resilient communities. This empowerment at the grassroots level is a catalyst for positive social change.

Cultural and gender empowerment is an essential aspect of societal progress. Empowering individuals from marginalized or underrepresented groups involves dismantling systemic barriers and promoting equal opportunities. This may require policy changes, advocacy, and concerted efforts to challenge ingrained stereotypes. The empowerment of women, for instance, is closely linked to economic development, improved health outcomes, and enhanced overall societal well-being.

The digital age has opened up new avenues for empowerment. Access to information technology, online learning platforms, and social media has democratized knowledge and connected people globally. Empowering others through digital means involves bridging the digital divide, ensuring equitable access to technology, and leveraging online platforms for education, collaboration, and advocacy.

Empowerment is not without challenges. Resistance to change, fear of failure, and ingrained power dynamics can impede progress. Overcoming these challenges requires a commitment to fostering a culture of continuous learning, adaptability, and resilience. It involves recognizing and addressing systemic inequalities that hinder empowerment, both on an individual and societal level.

In conclusion, empowering others is a multifaceted and dynamic process that involves recognizing and nurturing individual potential. It requires effective communication, education, mentorship, and a commitment to dismantling barriers that hinder progress. Empowerment is not a one-time event but an ongoing journey towards creating a more inclusive, just, and resilient world. Through empowerment, individuals can unlock their full potential, contributing to positive transformations in their lives and the broader community.

Emphasizing the Value of Women in Leadership

In recent years, there has been a growing recognition of the invaluable contributions that women bring to leadership roles across various sectors. This essay explores the significance of promoting and emphasizing the value of women in leadership positions, shedding light on the positive impact it can have on organizations and society as a whole.

Body:
Diversity and Inclusion:
Diversity in leadership brings a variety of perspectives, enhancing problem-solving and decision-making processes.
Inclusive leadership fosters a workplace culture that embraces differences, promoting creativity and innovation.
Different Leadership Styles:
Women often exhibit leadership styles that emphasize collaboration, empathy, and relationship-building.
A diverse leadership team incorporating both masculine and feminine leadership traits can lead to more balanced and effective outcomes.
Economic Benefits:
Studies suggest that companies with a higher representation of women in leadership positions tend to outperform their peers financially.
Diverse leadership can enhance a company's ability to understand and meet the needs of diverse consumer bases.
Role Modeling and Inspiration:
Women in leadership serve as role models for aspiring female professionals, inspiring confidence and ambition.
Increased visibility of women in leadership positions challenges stereotypes and encourages a shift in societal norms.
Enhanced Corporate Reputation:
Companies that prioritize gender diversity in leadership are often perceived as socially responsible and progressive.
Positive corporate reputation can attract top talent and appeal to a broader customer base.
Improved Organizational Culture:
Women leaders often contribute to a more inclusive and supportive organizational culture.
Addressing gender disparities fosters a healthier work environment, leading to increased employee satisfaction and retention.
Global Perspective:
Women leaders bring a global perspective, considering diverse cultural nuances and viewpoints.
In a globalized world, understanding and navigating cultural differences are crucial for successful leadership.
Breaking the Glass Ceiling:

Emphasizing the value of women in leadership challenges traditional gender norms and helps break the glass ceiling.
This fosters a sense of equality and fairness, promoting a more just and equitable society.

Conclusion:
In conclusion, emphasizing the value of women in leadership is not just a matter of equality but also a strategic imperative for organizations and society. Diverse leadership teams contribute to better decision-making, improved financial performance, and a more inclusive workplace culture. By recognizing and promoting the unique qualities that women bring to leadership roles, we can create a more equitable and prosperous future for all.

Impactful Leadership Stories

Nelson Mandela: Transformational Leadership
Nelson Mandela's journey from prisoner to president showcases transformational leadership. His ability to unite a divided nation, forgive his oppressors, and steer South Africa towards reconciliation is a testament to the power of resilience and visionary leadership.
Steve Jobs: Visionary Leadership at Apple
Steve Jobs' leadership at Apple is often cited for its innovation and impact on the tech industry. His ability to envision groundbreaking products like the iPhone and iPad, coupled with his relentless pursuit of perfection, exemplifies visionary leadership that transformed Apple into one of the world's most influential companies.

Malala Yousafzai: Courageous Leadership for Education
Malala Yousafzai's advocacy for girls' education in Pakistan, despite facing grave threats, demonstrates courageous leadership. Her unwavering commitment to equality and education has inspired millions worldwide, showcasing the profound impact a single individual can have on global issues.

Elon Musk: Bold Decision-Making at SpaceX
Elon Musk's leadership at SpaceX demonstrates bold decision-making and a willingness to take risks. From the brink of bankruptcy to becoming a major player in the space industry, Musk's leadership style emphasizes innovation, resilience, and a determination to achieve ambitious goals.

Abigail Johnson: Empowering Leadership at Fidelity Investments
Abigail Johnson's leadership at Fidelity Investments is characterized by her commitment to employee development and empowerment. By fostering a culture that values diversity and inclusivity, Johnson has created an environment where individuals can thrive, contributing to the company's success.

Winston Churchill: Inspirational Leadership During World War II
Winston Churchill's leadership during World War II is often cited for its inspirational quality. His speeches and unwavering resolve provided strength and hope to the British people during a challenging period, illustrating the impact of inspirational leadership in times of crisis.

Indra Nooyi: Transformational Leadership at PepsiCo
Indra Nooyi's tenure as CEO of PepsiCo exemplifies transformational leadership. She led the company through a shift towards healthier products, demonstrating a commitment to corporate social responsibility and adapting to changing consumer preferences.
Jacinda Ardern: Compassionate Leadership in Crisis
Jacinda Ardern's response to the Christchurch mosque shootings and the COVID-19 pandemic showcases compassionate leadership. Her empathetic communication, decisive actions, and focus on unity have earned her praise for leading New Zealand through challenging times.
Martin Luther King Jr.: Visionary Leadership in the Civil Rights Movement

Martin Luther King Jr.'s leadership in the civil rights movement is iconic for its vision of equality and justice. His advocacy for nonviolent protest and his powerful speeches played a pivotal role in the advancements of civil rights in the United States.

Satya Nadella: Transformational Leadership at Microsoft
Satya Nadella's leadership at Microsoft is marked by a focus on cultural transformation and innovation. His emphasis on empathy, continuous learning, and adapting to industry shifts has revitalized Microsoft and positioned it as a leader in the tech industry.

These stories highlight diverse leadership styles and the profound impact leaders can have on individuals, organizations, and society as a whole. From visionaries and transformers to compassionate and inspirational figures, these leaders provide valuable lessons for aspiring leaders in various fields.

Addressing Gender Bias

Addressing gender bias is crucial for fostering equality and inclusivity in various aspects of society. From workplaces to educational institutions, and even within households, pervasive gender bias can hinder individual growth and perpetuate harmful stereotypes. This essay explores the multifaceted nature of gender bias, its impact on different spheres of life, and effective strategies to mitigate its influence.

Introduction:

Gender bias, often rooted in societal norms and historical stereotypes, manifests in numerous ways, contributing to inequality between men and women. This bias can be explicit or subtle, overt or covert, and it affects individuals from a young age, shaping their perceptions and opportunities.

Understanding Gender Bias:

At its core, gender bias involves preconceived notions and expectations based on an individual's gender. This bias can be seen in various forms, such as differential treatment, unequal opportunities, and the reinforcement of traditional gender roles. Stereotypes about men being assertive leaders and women being nurturing caregivers, for instance, can limit both genders' potential.

Impact on Education:

Gender bias can significantly impact education, affecting not only students but also shaping societal attitudes towards certain fields of study. Research has shown that girls may face stereotypes suggesting they are less proficient in subjects like mathematics and science, leading to a lack of encouragement to pursue careers in these fields. Similarly, boys might face bias in areas perceived as more 'feminine,' discouraging them from exploring diverse interests.

Workplace Disparities:

The workplace is another arena where gender bias is pervasive. Disparities in pay, unequal opportunities for advancement, and biased hiring practices all contribute to a gendered work environment. Breaking the glass ceiling remains a challenge for many women, with gender bias acting as a barrier to their professional growth.

Media Influence:

Media plays a significant role in perpetuating and challenging gender bias. Stereotypical portrayals of men and women in movies, television, and advertisements can reinforce societal expectations. Efforts to challenge and change these representations are essential for promoting diverse and realistic depictions of gender roles.

Intersectionality:

It is crucial to recognize that gender bias is not a standalone issue; it intersects with other forms of discrimination. Factors such as race, sexual orientation, and socioeconomic status further compound the challenges faced by individuals. Intersectionality must be considered when addressing gender bias to ensure inclusive solutions that cater to diverse experiences.

Challenging Unconscious Bias:

Unconscious bias, deeply ingrained in societal norms, is a significant contributor to gender bias. Raising awareness and implementing training programs to challenge these biases can be instrumental in creating a more inclusive environment. Organizations can adopt strategies like blind recruitment to minimize unconscious biases during hiring processes.

Promoting Gender-Neutral Education:

Addressing gender bias in education requires implementing reforms that promote equality from an early age. This includes incorporating gender-neutral curricula, ensuring equal opportunities for participation in extracurricular activities, and fostering a supportive environment that encourages all students to pursue their interests irrespective of gender stereotypes.

Corporate Initiatives:

In the corporate world, organizations can take proactive measures to address gender bias. This involves implementing policies that promote equal pay, providing mentorship programs for women, and establishing a culture that values diversity and inclusion. Recognizing and celebrating achievements without gender bias can contribute to a more equitable workplace.

Legal Frameworks:

Legal frameworks play a crucial role in addressing gender bias. Enforcing anti-discrimination laws and promoting policies that mandate gender equality can create a foundation for change. Governments and institutions must work collaboratively to ensure that legislation reflects the principles of fairness and equal opportunity for all genders.

Empowering Women:

Empowering women is a fundamental aspect of addressing gender bias. This involves providing opportunities for skill development, mentorship, and leadership training. Creating a supportive network for women to share experiences and strategies can foster a sense of community and resilience against gender bias.

Changing Cultural Norms:

Cultural norms deeply influence perceptions of gender roles. Challenging these norms involves engaging communities in open conversations about gender bias and its impact. Education campaigns, media literacy programs, and community initiatives can contribute to shifting cultural attitudes towards more equitable and inclusive perspectives on gender.

Parental Roles and Responsibilities:

Addressing gender bias starts at home, where parents play a pivotal role. Encouraging parents to share responsibilities equally, regardless of traditional gender roles, sets a positive example for children. This can lead to the development of a more egalitarian mindset from an early age, breaking the cycle of gender bias in future generations.

Conclusion:

In conclusion, addressing gender bias is a complex and multifaceted challenge that requires concerted efforts from individuals, communities, and institutions. By understanding the various forms of bias, recognizing its impact on different aspects of life, and implementing targeted strategies, societies can move towards a more equitable and inclusive future. The fight against gender bias is not just a matter of fairness; it is an essential step towards building a world where everyone has equal opportunities to thrive, irrespective of their gender.

Achieving Goals

Setting and achieving goals is an integral part of personal and professional growth. It provides a sense of direction, motivation, and fulfillment. In this exploration of goal achievement, we'll delve into the importance of goal-setting, effective strategies, and the psychological factors that contribute to successful outcomes.

1. The Significance of Goal-Setting

Goals act as a compass, guiding individuals towards a desired destination. Whether they are short-term or long-term, personal or professional, goals provide a framework for progress. Setting clear, specific, and measurable goals helps create focus and a sense of purpose.

2. SMART Goals

A widely embraced approach to goal-setting is the SMART criteria: Specific, Measurable, Achievable, Relevant, and Time-bound. Breaking down goals into these components enhances clarity and facilitates a more systematic approach to success. For instance, defining specific milestones and establishing a timeframe creates a roadmap that fosters accountability.

3. Motivation and Goal Pursuit

Motivation serves as the engine that drives goal pursuit. Understanding intrinsic and extrinsic motivators helps individuals tailor their approach to stay committed. Intrinsic motivation, stemming from personal satisfaction and fulfillment, often proves more sustainable than external rewards.

4. Overcoming Obstacles

Challenges are inevitable on the path to achieving goals. Developing resilience and a problem-solving mindset is crucial. Embracing setbacks as learning opportunities and adjusting strategies when needed contributes to a more resilient and adaptable journey.

5. Goal Visualization and Affirmations

Visualization techniques and positive affirmations can play a significant role in achieving goals. By mentally picturing success and reinforcing belief in one's capabilities, individuals can enhance self-efficacy and increase the likelihood of goal attainment.

6. Time Management

Efficient time management is a key factor in achieving goals. Prioritizing tasks, setting deadlines, and minimizing distractions create a conducive environment for progress. Adopting time management tools and techniques can enhance productivity and keep individuals on track.

7. Accountability and Support Systems

Accountability is a powerful motivator. Sharing goals with others, whether through mentors, friends, or support groups, can provide encouragement and a sense of responsibility. Regular check-ins and feedback loops contribute to staying on course.

8. Continuous Learning and Adaptation

Flexibility and a willingness to learn are vital for goal achievement. Circumstances and priorities may change, requiring individuals to adapt their strategies. Continuous learning not only enhances skills but also fosters a growth mindset that thrives on challenges.

9. Celebrating Milestones

Acknowledging and celebrating milestones, no matter how small, is crucial for maintaining motivation. Recognizing progress reinforces the value of effort and serves as a reminder of the journey's significance.

10. Psychological Factors in Goal Achievement

Understanding psychological factors, such as self-efficacy, locus of control, and the impact of mindset, is essential. A growth mindset, believing in one's ability to develop skills, contributes significantly to overcoming obstacles and achieving challenging goals.

11. Balancing Multiple Goals

In a dynamic world, individuals often juggle multiple goals. Balancing competing priorities requires effective prioritization, organization, and the ability to allocate resources wisely.

12. Goal Reflection and Revision

Regularly reflecting on goals and their alignment with evolving values and aspirations is crucial. It allows individuals to assess progress, identify areas for improvement, and, if necessary, revise goals to better align with their current circumstances and ambitions.

In conclusion, achieving goals is a multifaceted journey that involves strategic planning, perseverance, and a deep understanding of oneself. By setting SMART goals, staying motivated, overcoming obstacles, and embracing continuous learning, individuals can navigate the path to success. Cultivating a resilient mindset, seeking support, and celebrating achievements contribute to a fulfilling and sustainable goal achievement process.

Creating a Positive Work Environment

Creating a positive work environment is crucial for fostering employee well-being, satisfaction, and overall productivity. A positive workplace culture not only enhances the quality of work but also contributes to employee retention and organizational success. In this exploration, we will delve into various aspects of cultivating a positive work environment, encompassing leadership, communication, recognition, work-life balance, and employee development.

1. Leadership and Management:
Leaders play a pivotal role in shaping the work environment. Transparent and empathetic leadership fosters trust and open communication. Leaders should exemplify the values they wish to instill in the workplace, setting a positive tone for the entire organization. Encouraging feedback and actively listening to employee concerns builds a sense of inclusion and shared responsibility.

2. Effective Communication:
Clear and open communication is the backbone of a positive work environment. Regular team meetings, feedback sessions, and transparent information sharing contribute to a sense of belonging and understanding among team members. Encouraging open dialogue helps address issues promptly, preventing misunderstandings and promoting a collaborative atmosphere.

3. Recognition and Appreciation:
Acknowledging and appreciating employees for their contributions is vital. Recognition can take various forms, from verbal praise to formal awards. Celebrating achievements, both big and small, creates a positive reinforcement loop, motivating employees to invest in their work and feel valued within the organization.

4. Work-Life Balance:
Balancing professional and personal life is integral to employee well-being. Encouraging reasonable working hours, providing flexible schedules, and promoting the importance of taking breaks contribute to a healthier work-life balance. This approach not only enhances job satisfaction but also prevents burnout, ultimately benefiting both individuals and the organization.

5. Employee Development:
Investing in the professional development of employees demonstrates a commitment to their growth. Offering training programs, mentorship opportunities, and career advancement paths empower employees to enhance their skills and contribute more effectively to the organization. This, in turn, boosts morale and job satisfaction.

6. Inclusivity and Diversity:
A positive work environment embraces diversity and fosters inclusivity. Cultivating a culture that values differences in perspectives, backgrounds, and experiences enhances creativity and innovation. Establishing policies that promote diversity and inclusion creates a sense of belonging for all employees, leading to a more harmonious workplace.

7. Flexible Work Arrangements:
Providing flexibility in work arrangements, such as remote work options or compressed workweeks, accommodates diverse lifestyles and preferences. This flexibility demonstrates trust in employees' ability to manage their responsibilities, leading to increased job satisfaction and a positive perception of the workplace.

8. Health and Wellness Programs:

Supporting employee well-being goes beyond the professional realm. Implementing health and wellness programs, such as fitness initiatives, mental health resources, and ergonomic workspaces, contributes to a holistic approach to employee care. Healthy employees are more likely to be engaged, focused, and productive.

9. Constructive Feedback and Growth Opportunities:
Regular performance feedback, focused on growth rather than criticism, is essential for employee development. Constructive feedback helps individuals understand their strengths and areas for improvement, fostering a continuous improvement mindset. Providing clear growth opportunities ensures that employees feel invested in their professional journey within the organization.

10. Team Building Activities:
Organizing team-building activities fosters camaraderie and a sense of community among employees. These activities can range from casual social events to more structured team-building exercises. Strengthening interpersonal relationships contributes to a positive and collaborative work environment.

In conclusion, creating a positive work environment is a multifaceted endeavor that requires a holistic approach. From leadership and communication to recognition and well-being initiatives, each component plays a crucial role in shaping the workplace culture. By prioritizing these elements, organizations can cultivate an atmosphere that promotes employee satisfaction, engagement, and ultimately, long-term success.

Results - Oriented Leadership

Results-oriented leadership is a management approach that prioritizes achieving measurable outcomes and tangible goals. This leadership style emphasizes delivering concrete results rather than merely focusing on processes or activities. Leaders who adopt a results-oriented approach are driven by a relentless commitment to achieving objectives and creating value for their organization. In this essay, we will explore the key principles, characteristics, and benefits of results-oriented leadership, as well as its potential challenges and the role it plays in today's dynamic business environment.

At its core, results-oriented leadership requires a clear and strategic vision. Leaders must articulate a compelling mission and set specific, measurable, achievable, relevant, and time-bound (SMART) goals for their teams. This clarity ensures that everyone in the organization understands the desired outcomes and can align their efforts accordingly. By establishing a roadmap for success, leaders provide a framework that guides decision-making and actions at all levels.

One of the fundamental characteristics of results-oriented leaders is their emphasis on accountability. They create a culture where individuals take ownership of their responsibilities and are answerable for the results they produce. This accountability fosters a sense of ownership and responsibility among team members, driving them to go above and beyond to meet or exceed expectations.

Effective communication is another cornerstone of results-oriented leadership. Leaders must communicate the organization's objectives clearly and consistently, ensuring that every team member understands their role in achieving these goals. Transparent communication fosters a shared understanding of expectations and encourages collaboration, aligning individual efforts with the overarching vision.

Adaptability is a crucial trait for results-oriented leaders. In today's rapidly changing business landscape, unforeseen challenges and opportunities arise regularly. Leaders must be flexible and able to adjust strategies to navigate unexpected obstacles. This ability to adapt ensures that the focus remains on achieving results despite external factors. Results-oriented leadership is closely tied to performance management. Leaders in this style prioritize evaluating and measuring outcomes regularly. They use key performance indicators (KPIs) to track progress, identify areas for improvement, and make data-driven decisions. By emphasizing performance evaluation, leaders can provide constructive feedback, recognize achievements, and address issues promptly to keep the team on course.

Motivating and inspiring teams is an essential aspect of results-oriented leadership. Leaders must understand the unique strengths and abilities of their team members and leverage this knowledge to foster a positive and productive work environment. Recognizing and celebrating individual and collective successes enhances morale and reinforces the commitment to achieving results.

The benefits of results-oriented leadership are numerous. Perhaps most importantly, this approach aligns organizational efforts with strategic goals, driving overall success. The emphasis on accountability fosters a culture of responsibility and ownership, leading to increased productivity and efficiency. Clear communication and transparency create a shared sense of purpose, enhancing teamwork and collaboration.

In addition to these advantages, results-oriented leadership often leads to innovation. The focus on outcomes encourages a mindset of continuous improvement, where team members are motivated to find creative solutions to challenges. The adaptability of results-oriented leaders allows for experimentation and learning from both successes and failures, fostering a culture of innovation within the organization.

However, despite its many benefits, results-oriented leadership is not without challenges. The relentless pursuit of outcomes may create a high-pressure environment, potentially leading to stress and burnout among team members. Leaders must balance the drive for results with a consideration for the well-being of their teams, implementing measures to support work-life balance and mental health.

Another challenge lies in finding the right balance between short-term and long-term goals. While results-oriented leaders are focused on achieving immediate objectives, they must also consider the broader strategic vision of the organization. It's essential to avoid sacrificing long-term sustainability for short-term gains, ensuring that results align with the organization's overall mission and values.

In today's dynamic business environment, characterized by rapid technological advancements and global competition, results-oriented leadership is more relevant than ever. Organizations need leaders who can navigate complexity, drive innovation, and deliver tangible outcomes. The ability to adapt to change, communicate effectively, and inspire teams to achieve results positions results-oriented leaders as valuable assets in the pursuit of organizational success.

In conclusion, results-oriented leadership is a management approach that prioritizes achieving measurable outcomes and tangible goals. Grounded in clear vision, accountability, adaptability, and effective communication, this leadership style fosters a culture of performance and innovation. While it brings numerous benefits.

Conclusion

In conclusion, the notion that women rule better in power is a complex and nuanced topic that encompasses various aspects of leadership, empathy, and inclusivity. While it is essential to avoid generalizations and recognize the diversity of leadership styles among individuals, there is evidence suggesting that women, on average, bring unique qualities to positions of power that can contribute positively to governance.

One key aspect is the emphasis on empathy and relational leadership. Research indicates that women often exhibit higher levels of emotional intelligence, allowing them to navigate interpersonal relationships with a greater understanding of others' perspectives. This emotional intelligence can foster collaboration, effective communication, and a more inclusive decision-making process. By prioritizing empathy, women leaders may create environments that are not only productive but also supportive and conducive to the well-being of individuals within the organization.

Moreover, studies have shown that women in leadership positions are more likely to champion diversity and inclusivity. This commitment to diversity can result in a broad range of perspectives being considered, leading to more innovative and well-rounded solutions to complex problems. In a world that increasingly values diversity, women leaders may be better positioned to navigate the challenges of a globalized and interconnected society.

Furthermore, women leaders often demonstrate a collaborative leadership style, seeking input from various stakeholders and building consensus. This approach contrasts with more autocratic or hierarchical leadership styles, potentially fostering a more participatory and democratic decision-making process. In a world facing intricate challenges that require multifaceted solutions, a leadership style that encourages collaboration and collective problem-solving may prove to be particularly effective.

It is important to note that attributing leadership qualities solely to gender oversimplifies the issue. Men and women can embody a range of leadership styles, and effective leadership is ultimately a result of individual characteristics, experiences, and skills. However, acknowledging the potential benefits associated with women in power does not diminish the accomplishments of male leaders. Rather, it encourages a more inclusive and diverse approach to leadership.

In conclusion, the idea that women rule better in power is rooted in the recognition of certain qualities that women, on average, bring to leadership positions. These qualities include heightened emotional intelligence, a commitment to diversity and inclusivity, and a collaborative leadership style. While these attributes are not exclusive to women, promoting gender diversity in leadership roles may contribute to a more balanced and effective approach to governance. As we move forward, it is crucial to recognize and celebrate the diverse strengths that individuals, irrespective of gender, bring to leadership, fostering a culture that values equality and inclusivity in all spheres of society.